D1716800

Presented To
Murrell Memorial Library

by

John Ashford

2010

The **Missouri** River

by Leon Gray

Gareth Stevens Publishing
A WORLD ALMANAC EDUCATION GROUP COMPANY

Please visit our web site at: www.garethstevens.com
For a free color catalog describing Gareth Stevens Publishing's list of high-quality
books and multimedia programs, call 1-800-542-2595 (USA) or 1-800-387-3178
(Canada). Gareth Stevens Publishing's fax: (414) 332-3567.

Library of Congress Cataloging-in-Publication Data

Gray, Leon.
    The Missouri River / by Leon Gray.
       p. cm. — (Rivers of North America)
    Includes bibliographical references and index.
    Contents: Big Muddy—From source to mouth—The life of the river—On the Wild Frontier—
Taming the Plains—Places to visit—How rivers form.
    ISBN 0-8368-3758-4 (lib. bdg.)
    1. Missouri River—Juvenile literature. [1. Missouri River.] I. Title. II. Series.
F598.G73 2003
978—dc21   2003043918

This North American edition first published in 2004 by
Gareth Stevens Publishing
A World Almanac Education Group Company
330 West Olive Street, Suite 100
Milwaukee, Wisconsin 53212 USA

Original copyright © 2004 The Brown Reference Group plc. This U.S. edition copyright © 2004
by Gareth Stevens, Inc.

Author: Leon Gray
Editor: Tom Jackson
Consultant: Judy Wheatley Maben, Education Director, Water Education Foundation
Designer: Steve Wilson
Cartographer: Mark Walker
Picture Researcher: Clare Newman
Indexer: Kay Ollerenshaw
Managing Editor: Bridget Giles
Art Director: Dave Goodman

Gareth Stevens Editor: Betsy Rasmussen
Gareth Stevens Designer: Melissa Valuch

Picture Credits: Cover: Whitecliff region of Missouri River in Montana. (Skyscan: Jim Wark)
Contents: A riverboat at Omaha, Nebraska, in the late 19th century.

Key: l–left, r–right, t–top, b–bottom.
Ardea: John Mason 13; P. Morris 11t; Bridgeman Art Library: 19; Corbis: 16b, 17; Bettmann 15; Digital
Stock 24t; Dave G. Houser 29l; Layne Kennedy 24b; David Muench 5r; Charles E. Rotkin 23; Scott T.
Smith 8; Getty Images: 18; Mary Evans Picture Library: 16t, 21; Missouri Division of Tourism: 4, 29br;
NASA: 9r; National Archives: 14, 20; PhotoDisc: D. Falconer/PhotoLink 27; Robert Hunt Library: 29tr;
Skyscan: J. Wark 7, 9l; Still Pictures: Peter Arnold/Alex S. MacLean 22; U.S. Fish & Wildlife Service: Ron
Singer 11b; R. Town 10; U.S. Army Corps of Engineers: 25t, 25b; Robert Etzel 12; Harry Weddington 5l, 26

Printed in the United States of America

1 2 3 4 5 6 7 8 9 07 06 05 04 03

Table of Contents

Big Muddy

The Missouri River used to flood so often and wash away so much soil that it was nicknamed "Big Muddy." Dams and channels have changed the Missouri for good.

At 2,315 miles (3,725 kilometers) long, the Missouri River takes the prize for the longest river in North America. This powerful watercourse starts life in the Rocky Mountains of northwestern Montana. It cuts through the vast expanse of the Great Plains before turning east and discharging into North America's other mighty river—the Mississippi.

Raging River

When the first Europeans arrived in North America, few rivers were as powerful as the Missouri. Driven by the seasonal meltwaters from the snowcapped Rockies, the Missouri River twisted and turned through the heart of America, eroding riverbanks, carving new channels, tearing down trees, and washing over huge areas of floodplain. Today, the river's water is controlled by several dams.

People of the Missouri

The Missouri River has been a lifeline for people for thousands of years. Native people grew crops along the Missouri's banks, took

Left: *The Gateway Arch in St. Louis, Missouri, was built to celebrate the many pioneers who traveled west along the nearby Missouri River.*

Right: *The Gates of the Mountains, near the Missouri's source in Montana.*

Below: *Gavin's Point Dam crosses the Missouri River between South Dakota and Nebraska.*

fish from the river, and ventured onto the open prairies of the Great Plains to hunt bison.

Today, several large cities stand along the Missouri's banks. Many developed as staging posts for thousands of European settlers spreading west in search of new homes or a fortune.

A River Tamed

Many of the people living beside the Missouri River work on farms or in food-processing plants. The river's cities have important ports that send the food downriver to other parts of the country.

Farming along the Missouri is not without its problems, however. Until the 1950s, flooding often ruined crops, damaged homes, and endangered the lives of the

farmers and their families. Today, the farms are protected by dams across the Missouri's upper reaches, and the river's fragile banks have been reinforced. The dams have created huge reservoirs that store the water, which would otherwise flood the fields. These lakes have become water sports centers, and the extra water is used to generate electricity and to irrigate crops.

While these flood controls have undoubtedly been good for people, they have their disadvantages. The dams prevent floodwaters from entering the Missouri Valley. The floods used to create habitats for wildlife and enrich the soil beside the river. Some wildlife is now close to extinction, but conservationists are working to return parts of the Missouri River to their natural state.

From Source to Mouth

From its source high in the Rocky Mountains to its meeting point with the Mississippi River, the Missouri River winds its way through the wide open prairies of the Great Plains.

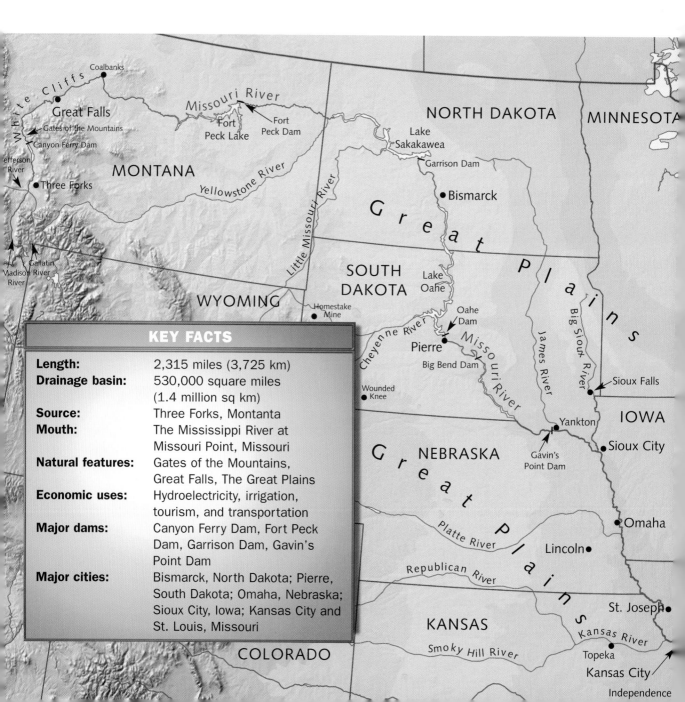

KEY FACTS

Length:	2,315 miles (3,725 km)
Drainage basin:	530,000 square miles (1.4 million sq km)
Source:	Three Forks, Montanta
Mouth:	The Mississippi River at Missouri Point, Missouri
Natural features:	Gates of the Mountains, Great Falls, The Great Plains
Economic uses:	Hydroelectricity, irrigation, tourism, and transportation
Major dams:	Canyon Ferry Dam, Fort Peck Dam, Garrison Dam, Gavin's Point Dam
Major cities:	Bismarck, North Dakota; Pierre, South Dakota; Omaha, Nebraska; Sioux City, Iowa; Kansas City and St. Louis, Missouri

Map labels: Coalbanks, White Cliffs, Great Falls, Gates of the Mountains, Canyon Ferry Dam, Jefferson River, Three Forks, Gallatin River, Madison River, MONTANA, Missouri River, Fort Peck Lake, Fort Peck Dam, Yellowstone River, Little Missouri River, NORTH DAKOTA, MINNESOTA, Lake Sakakawea, Garrison Dam, Bismarck, Great Plains, SOUTH DAKOTA, Lake Oahe, WYOMING, Homestake Mine, Cheyenne River, Oahe Dam, Pierre, Missouri River, Big Bend Dam, James River, Big Sioux River, Sioux Falls, IOWA, Wounded Knee, Yankton, Gavin's Point Dam, Sioux City, NEBRASKA, Great Plains, Platte River, Omaha, Lincoln, Republican River, St. Joseph, KANSAS, Kansas River, Smoky Hill River, Topeka, Kansas City, Independence, COLORADO

The Missouri is the longest river in the United States, traveling a total course of 2,315 miles (3,725 km) from its source at Three Forks, Montana, to Missouri Point, Missouri, where it joins the Mississippi River. The river drains about 530,000 square miles (1.4 million sq km) of land—one-sixth of the total area of the United States and a large part of Canada.

The Long Journey Begins

The Missouri River forms where the Gallatin, Jefferson, and Madison Rivers meet at Three Forks, Montana. From Three Forks, the Missouri winds through the White Cliffs region of Montana, which is named for the steep valley cut by the river. Fifty miles (80 km) from its source, the Missouri meets Canyon Ferry Dam. This is the first of several huge dams that cross the river's upper section.

Continuing northward, the Missouri passes through the Gates of the Mountains, a narrow canyon with almost vertical walls rising 1,200 feet (365 meters) above the river. Soon after, the river flows through the city of Great Falls, Montana. There,

PARKS AND FORESTS

- Big Muddy National Wildlife Refuge, Missouri
- Lewis and Clark National Historic Trail
- Little Missouri National Grassland, North Dakota
- Missouri National Recreational River, South Dakota and Nebraska
- Ozark National Scenic Riverways, Missouri
- Theodore Roosevelt National Park, North Dakota

WISCONSIN

TRIBUTARIES

- Big Sioux
- Cheyenne
- James
- Kansas
- Little Missouri
- Platte
- Yellowstone

Milwaukee

Chicago

ILLINOIS

MISSOURI

Mississippi River

Illinois River

Missouri River

Missouri Point

St. Louis

Osage River

Jefferson City

es ines

Below: *The Missouri River flows into the Mississippi at Missouri Point north of St. Louis, Missouri.*

7

Above: *The Eye of the Needle was a natural arch in the White Cliffs region of the Missouri River in Montana. In 1997, vandals knocked it down.*

North Dakota. Then, the Missouri is joined by the Yellowstone River—its largest tributary—and widens into Lake Sakakawea. This great reservoir is held back by Garrison Dam. From this point, the Missouri River heads south to Bismarck, North Dakota's capital, and on to Lake Oahe, which straddles the border with South Dakota.

On the South Dakota side of Lake Oahe, the Cheyenne River joins the Missouri. Past Pierre, South Dakota, the Missouri River turns southeast and forms the boundary between South Dakota and Nebraska.

At Yankton, South Dakota, the river passes though Gavin's Point Dam, the last on the Missouri. The river is then met by the James River before continuing on to Sioux City, Iowa. From there, the Missouri forms the state line between Nebraska and Iowa.

the Missouri cascades over five waterfalls, dropping more than 400 feet (120 m) in 12 miles (19 km). Great Falls is called "Electric City" because its power plants make electricity from the river's strong current.

The Missouri River then turns east and widens into the enormous Fort Peck Lake. This reservoir is formed by Fort Peck Dam—one of the largest in the world.

Great Plains Country
Beyond Fort Peck Lake, the Missouri River flows into

The Lower Stretch
The lower stretch of the Missouri River, a 735-mile (1,190-km) section from Sioux City to the Mississippi, has been turned into a narrow, 9-foot (2.75-m) deep channel used by barges. Turning south from Sioux City, the river is joined by the Platte River just south of Omaha, Nebraska. The

Missouri then forms another short state boundary between Nebraska and Missouri and again between Kansas and Missouri until it reaches Kansas City, Missouri—the largest metropolitan area along the Missouri River. The Kansas River joins the Missouri at Kansas City, and the river then turns sharply eastward, across the central part of the state of Missouri. The river finally empties into the Mississippi at Missouri Point, a few miles north of St. Louis, Missouri.

Before the Dams

Long before it was tamed by dams and channels, the Missouri changed often. Much of the river was frozen in the winter. In the spring and early summer, increased rainfall and melting snow from the Rocky Mountains and the prairies caused large floods. These water surges would wash away the riverbanks, tear down trees, and carve new channels out of the loose soils of the Great Plains. The river carried so much brown soil it was nicknamed "Big Muddy."

River of Change

Dams have transformed the Missouri. Today, floodwater is captured in reservoirs. It is then let out slowly, to stop water from surging over the banks downstream. Big Muddy's water is now much clearer because the soil settles out in the calm lakes. Most of the Missouri's banks are also reinforced with earth and stone levees, which prevent them from being washed away.

Below Right: *The southern half of Lake Oahe snakes through the farmland of South Dakota. This image was taken by a satellite looking to the south.*

Below Left: *The Missouri River meanders through the mountains west of Great Falls, Montana.*

Oahe Dam

SOUTH

DAKOTA

N

2 The Life of the River

The Missouri River's wildlife once lived compatibly with the yearly floods. Now the plants and animals are having to find new ways to survive in the tamed Missouri River.

Despite all the damage they do, floods are good for rivers and their wildlife. As the fast-moving floodwater washes over the banks, it collects dirt and mud. The mud settles on the surrounding land and forms a layer of fertile soil. The floods also build new habitats, such as sandbars, channels, marshes, and lakes. This creates a wide variety of places where river wildlife can feed, shelter, and breed.

Below: *A muskrat feeds on a shallow reed bed. These rodents shelter in burrows in the banks of the Missouri and its tributaries.*

The Original Missouri

When the first Europeans settled by the Missouri River, they encountered a landscape different from what is there today. On both sides of the river, a dense forest of ash, box elder, cottonwood, elm, oak, and willow stretched over the floodplain. Beneath the forest, countless flowers carpeted the land. Plants such as honeysuckle, serviceberry, and wild grape also thrived.

CATFISH IN THE MISSOURI

There are three main species of catfish in the Missouri River: the blue catfish, channel catfish, and flathead catfish (below). All have smooth, scaleless skin, flattened heads, and pairs of long, whiskerlike barbels on their chins. These barbels help the fish feel their way around murky river bottoms. During the day, catfish shelter in natural hollows, under logs, and in deep pools. At night, they come out to feed on crayfish, insects, mollusks, aquatic plants, and smaller fish.

Missouri River catfish have long been highly prized by fishers, who enjoy eating as well as catching them. Catfish are less common in the river today because dams have destroyed their habitat. There are about half the number of catfish in the river than fifty years ago and almost none at all in some parts of the river.

In an attempt to restore the dwindling populations, only a few fishers are allowed to fish each year. In just ten years, catfish populations have steadily increased, so these measures seem to be working.

During the spring floods, some of the trees that lined the Missouri were washed into the river and became stuck in shallow channels or behind sandbars. As these trees rotted away, they were eaten by insect larvae and other small aquatic animals. In turn, these tiny animals provided food for many types of fish, frogs, turtles, and waterbirds.

The forest beside the river was home to a wide range of animals, from grizzly bears and timber wolves to raccoons and white-tailed deer. Smaller animals, such as beavers, mink, muskrat, and otters, made their homes along the riverbanks and up small side creeks.

Great Plains

As the Missouri traveled east, the forest gave way to a vast prairie called the Great Plains. The animals and plants that lived on the Great Plains had to be tough to survive the region's bitterly cold winters and hot summers. The Great Plains were covered by a sea of grasses mixed with larger

Right: *River otters did not do well after the Missouri was dammed. Today, however, conservationists have managed to restore the otter population.*

SANDBAR HABITATS

Interior least terns and piping plovers only nest on sandbars in the Missouri River. Before the dams were built, sandbars supported many of these nesting waterbirds. The dams now stop the yearly floods that would make new sandbars. Today, the birds have very few places to breed. As a result, the interior least tern and the piping plover are nearly extinct in the United States. Most people agree that the best way to help these birds is to preserve existing sandbar habitats and create new sandbars on the Missouri River. Releasing water from dams more often could create new sandbars, but it has been difficult to coordinate this with the interests of other river users.

Above: A pair of interior least terns nest on a sandbar below Gavin's Point Dam in South Dakota.

plants, such as yuccas and prickly pears. The Great Plains were home to huge herds of grazing mammals, such as bison, deer, and pronghorn. Other grassland animals included coyotes, jackrabbits, grouse, prairie dogs, and rattlesnakes.

Human Impact

The Missouri's floods are now controlled by the dams in the upper stretch of the river. The animals and plants of the Missouri River have paid a high price for this. The dams put an end to the high water levels that once triggered the breeding of river fish. Because of this, the numbers of fish, such as sturgeon, chub, and catfish, have been going down. The pallid sturgeon, for example, is now close to extinction.

Many of the river's forests have been cut down, and farms now take their place. Because of this, fewer trees are washed into the river. Since dead trees are a crucial food for tiny animals, the loss of the forests have had an effect on the community of animals in the river.

Birds that used to nest in the forest have also been affected. For example, just a handful of nesting bald eagles now rely on the riverside woodlands. Many other birds of prey are less common than before.

While Native people hunting did not have a large effect on the population of bison, later settlers hunted them to near extinction. Today, only small herds remain in preserves.

Looking to the Future

Fortunately, conservationists are working hard to help the river's wildlife. There are many success stories. For example, river otters were once trapped for their fur, and they fell in number. Now, they have been successfully brought back to the river.

Although some wildlife has suffered since the dams were built, the dams also created new habitats. Waterbirds use the dam's reservoirs to rest on their migrations. Many lakes have fish hatcheries, which breed native fish, such as pallid sturgeon, and introduce them into the river.

Below: *A prickly pear flowers on the prairie. This cactus is one of the few nongrass plants that grow naturally on the Great Plains.*

3 On the Wild Frontier

The Missouri River was the main route into the Great Plains. Many pioneers followed the river, heading for a new life in the West. The Native Plains people, however, did not welcome them.

Above: *A group of Arapaho perform a "ghost dance" at the end of the nineteenth century. The Arapaho and other Native people believed that these dances would drive non-Native settlers away.*

The lifestyle of the people that live near the Missouri River is influenced by the grassy plateau, known as the Great Plains. Before Spanish explorers brought horses to North America in the middle of the seventeenth century, Native people lived mainly in villages along the Missouri and its tributaries. Groups such as the Hidatsa, Omaha, Osage, and Mandan lived in lodges made of earth.

The Missouri, Kaw, Oto, and Iowa built huge tents of buffalo hide called tepees.

The Missouri's people grew corn and other food crops and took fish from the rivers. Hunting parties left the river in search of animals such as pronghorn, white-tailed deer, and bison. The hunters sheltered in smaller tents and relied on dogs to drag their equipment on A-shaped sleds.

Hunting bison on foot was hard work. Many hunters relied on stealth, silently killing one or two animals without scaring the herd. Another tactic was to startle the buffalo, causing them to stampede. The hunters could then drive the herd over a cliff.

Buildings near St. Joseph, Missouri, submerged by the floods of 1952.

THE GREAT FLOOD OF 1952

The great Missouri flood of 1952 was one of the most devastating in the river's history. Between April 12 and June 29, 1952, more than 100,000 people were evacuated from their homes as the floodwaters covered farms and towns from Sioux City, Iowa, south to Kansas City, Missouri. At the peak of the flood, the swollen watercourse rose to 31.5 feet (9.6 m)—nearly 15 feet (4.6 m) above its normal high-water level. At various points along the river, the Missouri measured a staggering 15 miles (24 km) across. President Harry S. Truman (1884–1972) declared an official state of emergency and ordered U.S. Army troops to reinforce the artificial riverbanks, or levees, and build refugee camps to house the growing number of homeless. When the floodwaters eventually subsided, the Army Corps of Engineers put the damage at an estimated $11.9 million. One of the only good things about the great flood of 1952 was that few people died because people had been warned in advance to leave the most dangerous areas.

Changing Cultures

After horses were brought to North America from Europe, some Native groups, such as the Arapaho, Crow Comanche, and Sioux, adopted a nomadic way of life, regularly moving from place to place. They became expert riders and skilled mounted hunters, especially after they began using rifles. Hunts, and then wars with the United States, were marked by rituals and dances for good luck. The hunters painted their bodies with charcoal, clay, and the juice of brightly colored berries.

The men and women of these nomadic groups made different contributions to the community. The men hunted, made weapons, and protected the camp. The women did all the other jobs. They cut the meat into thin strips ready for drying. They made bedding, clothes, and tepees from animal hides and embroidered clothes with dyed porcupine quills. They also packed up the camp before the group moved on.

The Frontier

French explorers Jacques Marquette and Louis Jolliet came across the mouth of the Missouri River in 1673 as they traveled down the Mississippi River. Fur traders began making trips upstream, but the first careful exploration of the river was made by Etienne Veniard de Bourgmont. In 1714, he traveled a short distance from the Mississippi River to the mouth of the Platte River. In the late eighteenth century, Pierre Gaultier de Verennes and his sons were

Left: *U.S. explorers Lewis and Clark arrive at the Great Falls in Montana.*

Below: *Native hunters kill bison as they swim across the Missouri River.*

THE CASE OF COW ISLAND

The Missouri River forms the state boundary between Kansas and Missouri. A flood in 1881 had unforeseen consequences for Charles Keane, the owner of a saloon on Cow Island on the Kansas side of the Missouri. The sheer volume of floodwater changed the course of the river. When the flood subsided, Cow Island—and Keane's saloon—were located on the Missouri side of the river. The sale of liquor was legal in Kansas, but state laws in Missouri prohibited it. Keane was duly arrested and convicted of this offense. However, Keane appealed and was let off. The appeal court held that a sudden shift of the channel did not mean that the state boundary changed with it. Consequently, the state boundary remained where it had been before the flood. Keane's release was welcomed by many thirsty Missouri residents, who could now travel home from the saloon without having to cross the wide river.

Above: *Saloon customers from the late nineteenth century enjoy a game.*

the first to follow the river into what is now South Dakota. His sons left a plaque recording the visit near where the city of Pierre stands today.

Westward Bound

Captain Meriwether Lewis and Lieutenant William Clark were the first U.S. citizens to travel the whole length of the Missouri River between 1804 and 1806. President Thomas Jefferson wanted to find a route across North America to the Pacific Ocean. He asked Lewis to lead the expedition, and Lewis invited his friend Clark to accompany him as joint leader. On May 14, 1804, the pair set off from St. Louis with forty men.

Six months later, Lewis and Clark set up a winter camp

across the river from a Native village, near the present site of Bismarck, North Dakota. They built a small fort—named Fort Mandan in honor of their Native hosts—and waited until the weather got warmer. At Fort Mandan, the group met a French mountain man named Toussaint Charbonneau and his Shoshone wife Sacagawea. The couple joined the expedition, and in April 1805, the group resumed their journey up the Missouri River, passing the mouth of the Yellowstone River a few weeks later. The group had to carry their equipment around the Great Falls in Montana, but they finally reached the Missouri's headwaters at Three Forks on July 25. From there, they continued over the Rockies and eventually reached the Pacific on November 7, 1805.

On September 23, 1806, Lewis and Clark arrived back at St. Louis. Their expedition was a huge success. Lewis, Clark, and many other members of the expedition brought back detailed journals and maps of the territory they crossed.

Blazing Trails

Soon more explorers, fur traders, missionaries, and pioneering settlers began to follow the trail blazed by Lewis and Clark. In 1817, the first steamboat—the *Zebulon Pike*—started up the river. It carried people as far as Independence, Westport (the early name for Kansas City), and St. Joseph in Missouri, where a big bend in the Missouri River veered to the northwest. These cities grew up in the early nineteenth century as the starting points for settlers heading for the West. The settlers left the cities along routes called the Oregon and Santa Fe Trails.

In turn, many new towns were established as supply centers and military outposts to supply and protect the

Below: *A painting from 1863 shows the city of Omaha, Nebraska, beside the Missouri.*

wagons on the trails. As steamboats traveled farther up the Missouri River, many more forts and trading posts appeared along the banks. Some of these settlements, such as those at Pierre and Yankton, have grown into today's urban centers.

Gold Fever

In 1848, another wave of migration along the Oregon and Santa Fe Trails occurred after gold was discovered nearly 1,700 miles (2,735 km) away in California. James Marshall found gold near the Sacramento River while he was building a sawmill for John Sutter. The two men became partners and tried to keep their discovery secret.

The news leaked out, however, and by the next year, 80,000 fortune seekers had traveled to the area. The California "gold rush" guaranteed the success of Independence, Kansas City, and St. Joseph because many of the miners traveled through these towns.

Fueling Development

The trails continued to be well traveled even after a railroad was built across the country in 1869. The coming of the railroads further fueled development west of the Missouri River. The railroad

INDEPENDENCE, MISSOURI

Independence, Missouri—the so-called "Queen City of the Trails"—developed as a trailhead early in the nineteenth century. Independence was ideal as the starting point for westbound overland traffic. The city is located where the Missouri River veers to the north, and so travelers heading west could not continue by boat. Having arrived by steamboat, travelers would load their belongings onto wagons that lined the square in the center of the city. Trains of wagons regularly left on long journeys west.

A trader named William Becknell had established the famous Santa Fe Trail in 1821. Independence became even busier when the Oregon Trail was opened in 1843. The city's prosperity was short-lived. A cholera epidemic devastated Independence in 1849, and the outbreak of the American Civil War in 1861 also took its toll. Independence ceased to be the river's most important town when Kansas City was chosen as the site of a Missouri–Pacific Railroad station in 1865. By this time, however, Independence was well established and remained one of the river's major cities.

companies were given vast areas of land on which to build their tracks.

Like the steamboats and trails before, the railroads stimulated the growth of many new settlements along

Above: *A wagon train heads west across a frozen river.*

the Missouri River. Bismarck, North Dakota, Omaha, Nebraska, and Sioux City, Iowa, all became important railroad hubs and transportation centers.

Not only did the railroad construction companies attract workers, they also sold their land to many more settlers, who brought new farming methods to the area. Where there was too little rainfall to support crops, the plains became grazing grounds for cattle.

Breeding Resentment

Many Native people on the Great Plains did not welcome European settlers to the Missouri River. Native peoples shared their land. All members of the groups used the land on which they lived, but no one individual owned it. The new arrivals followed European customs with plots of land having a single owner. The settlers put up fences and protected their land by force. Violent clashes between Natives and settlers took place as early as the 1630s. When the United States became independent from Britain in 1785, the new government began to move Native people from their homes. Several wars broke out when groups refused to move. Perhaps the most famous of these came in 1876, when the Sioux were told to leave the Black Hills near the Cheyenne River in South Dakota. Gold had been found in the hills, and miners wanted the land. The Sioux refused to go, and Lieutenant Colonel George Armstrong Custer was sent to force them out. Custer and

Below: *The steamboat Rosebud docked at Bismarck, North Dakota, in 1878. Before dams were built on the Missouri in the twentieth century, boats could travel all the way to Coalbanks, Montana.*

THE PONY EXPRESS

The owners of a freight and stagecoach company—the Central Overland California and Pikes Peak Express Company—founded the Pony Express in 1860. Their intent was to provide a fast mail delivery service between St. Joseph, Missouri, on the banks of the Missouri River, and Sacramento, California.

The journey was made by a continuous relay of riders. Riders got a new horse every 10 miles (16 km) or so. Every 60 miles (100 km), another rider took over. The entire journey took about ten days in summer and up to sixteen days in winter.

For nearly two years, the Pony Express was the fastest means of communication between the east and west coasts of the United States. The owners put hundreds of thousands of dollars into the venture in hopes of winning a one million dollar contract from the government. Political pressures and the outbreak of the Civil War (1861–1865) prevented the owners of the company from winning the contract. By the time the copper telegraph wires reached California late in 1861, the Pony Express was in financial ruin.

his men were wiped out by the Souix under the leadership of Sitting Bull. Eventually, however, the Sioux were defeated and made to live on reservations.

In 1890, many Indians began to perform religious rituals called "Ghost Dances." They believed the rituals would help them return the Great Plains to the way they once were. The Ghost Dance movement died out after three hundred Sioux were shot by the U.S. Army at Wounded Knee, South Dakota.

Into the New Century

By the twentieth century, farming had become the largest industry along the Missouri. Although most farms thrived, many suffered from the harsh weather, which sometimes destroyed crops, or the damaging effects of the river.

Between 1900 and 1952, ten major floods devastated farms and ranches along the riverbank. The Great Depression and drought of the 1930s were equally damaging, and addressing the problem became a matter of national interest. A number of dams were built along the Missouri in the 1950s and 1960s. The dams have provided flood control, hydroelectric power, and irrigation water ever since.

Above: *A Pony Express rider passes through a Native burial ground.*

4 Taming the Plains

Once the power of the Missouri River had been harnessed by a series of dams, the farms and cities along its banks began to benefit from irrigation water and cheap electricity.

Below: *A huge wheat farm stretches as far as the eye can see in northern Montana. The crops are irrigated with water from small tributaries of the Missouri River.*

As more and more people settled by the Missouri River, great cities grew along its banks. These city dwellers needed electricity for their homes and food for their families. They also needed protection from the great floods. Farmers transformed the river's floodplain forests and open prairie into fields to grow crops such as barley, corn, rye, soybeans, and wheat. After the herds of buffalo were cleared from the plains at the beginning of the twentieth century, ranchers began to raise cattle on the prairies.

To protect homes and farms from floods, engineers built several dams across the

GARRISON DAM

Situated 75 miles (120 km) upriver from Bismarck—the capital of North Dakota—Garrison Dam is the largest dam on the Missouri and the fifth largest in the United States. Nine million truckloads of earth were used to build the dam, which is 2.5 miles (4 km) long and nearly half a mile (0.8 km) wide at its base. The dam was started in 1947 and took another seven years—and $300 million—to complete.

Garrison Dam makes enough electricity to supply a city the size of Omaha, Nebraska. The dam also controls the Missouri's spring flood. The dam has created Lake Sakakawea, named for the Native woman met by Lewis and Clark in 1804. It is the third-largest reservoir in the United States. People use the lake for a range of water sports.

Missouri River and reinforced its banks with rocks and concrete. The huge dams also included power plants to generate electricity from the river's current. The water stored behind the dams in lakes was used to irrigate the region's crops. The dams also made the river calmer and deeper, and people were able to transport cargo in large barges all year-round.

Droughts and Floods
Before dams were built on the river, life was tough along the Missouri. Each year, floodwaters swamped the surrounding land, destroying homes and farms at a cost of millions of dollars.

Other parts of the Missouri Valley saw little water for most of the year. During the Great Depression of the 1930s, droughts turned fields into dry "dust bowls," and many farmers were forced to leave their land as the crops failed. In response to these droughts and floods, the U.S government decided to make sure that these problems could not damage the region again.

Above: *Lake Sakakawea stretches out behind Garrison Dam in North Dakota. Water is released from the lake down the dam's concrete spillway (foreground).*

THE HOMESTAKE MINE

For 125 years, the Homestake Mine in the Black Hills of South Dakota was the largest working gold mine in the United States. Vast gold deposits were uncovered during a gold rush of the 1870s. The Black Hills were part of a Sioux reservation when fortune seekers first struck gold there. The United States government offered to buy the land from the Sioux, but the Sioux refused to leave their reservation, and war broke out. The Sioux scored a few victories against the U.S. Army, such as the defeat of Lieutenant Colonel George Custer in the 1876 Battle of the Little Bighorn, but they eventually lost their land. Tens of thousands of people came to the region hoping to strike it rich.

The Homestake deposit turned out to be the most productive of all the mines in the Black Hills. Between 1876 and 2001, the mine produced one billion dollars worth of gold. The mine closed in 2001, but the government is considering whether or not to convert it into an underground laboratory where physicists can study atoms.

Below: *The Homestake Mine has formed a huge hole in the Black Hills of South Dakota.*

The Pick–Sloan Plan

William Glenn Sloan was in charge of the Bureau of Reclamation's work to set up irrigation projects in the area. He decided that dams were needed along the upper part of the Missouri River and its tributaries. At the same time, the U.S. Army Corps of Engineers was working to control the Missouri's floods, under General Lewis Pick. Pick's plan was to build levees from Sioux City to St. Louis and to build a series of dams on the main river. In 1944, the two plans were merged into the Pick–Sloan Plan.

Left: *A combine harvests a crop of wheat. The Missouri's water has turned the dry soil of the Great Plains into fertile farmland.*

Right: *The Big Bend Dam being constructed in the 1960s. The dam crosses the Missouri south of Pierre, South Dakota.*

Franklin D. Roosevelt, the president at the time, liked the plan because it would create jobs for soldiers returning from World War II (1939–1945), as well as solve the river's many problems.

Enacting the Plan

Between 1945 and 1966, six dams were built across the upper section of the Missouri at a cost of 1.2 billion dollars. The first, Canyon Ferry Dam, is in Montana and the last, Gavin's Point Dam, is in Nebraska. The giant Fort Peck Dam in Montana was built in 1936. It is one of the largest earth-filled dams in the world, with more than one billion cubic yards (7.6 million cubic m) of soil in its embankment. After the Pick–Sloan plan was enacted, Fort Peck became the second-largest dam on the Missouri.

As well as providing water to irrigate many thousands of square miles (sq km) of farmland along the Missouri River, the dams generate

Above: *A huge funnel is built at the base of Big Bend Dam. Once it was finished, river water surged through this funnel from the electricity plant inside the dam.*

electricity for tens of thousands of homes along the upper section of the river. Hydroelectric power plants are cheaper to run and produce less pollution than power plants that burn fuels, such as gas or coal.

Besides dams, strong levees were built along the Missouri's banks to stop floodwater from washing onto the land. The levees also made it easier for barge traffic to travel up and down the lower part of the river. Barges, however, can no longer travel upstream from Gavin's Point Dam, so traffic is limited to between Sioux City and St. Louis. There are

other large river ports at Omaha and Kansas City. As well as grain and other foods, the river's barges also carry raw materials to factories in the cities and take away the products made in them.

Pros and Cons
The construction of so many dams has changed the Missouri River in many ways. Farmers reap huge rewards from the constant supply of water trapped in the river's enormous reservoirs. The Missouri River provides businesses with cheap electricity and is a useful waterway for

Above: *Barges are pushed up the Missouri River near Omaha, Nebraska.*

THE HEART OF AMERICA

Because it lies close to the center of the United States, Kansas City, Missouri, is often called the "Heart of America." It is the largest urban area on the Missouri River, being home to more than half a million people. Kansas City stands where the Kansas River meets the Missouri. It straddles the border between Kansas and Missouri, but most of the city, including the downtown district, is in Missouri.

Kansas City began as a small trading post in 1821. The post was founded by French fur trader Francois Chouteau. Within a few years, the settlement was the starting point for many pioneers heading west on the Oregon and Santa Fe Trails. The railroad arrived there in 1865, and Hannibal Bridge—the first across the Missouri—was built in 1869.

Kansas City was soon a bustling commercial center, with a large livestock market. Today, the city is still one of the most important livestock and crop markets in the United States. Produce from farms in Kansas—the country's greatest wheat-producing state—is carried to the city on the Missouri and Kansas Rivers. Food-processing plants are common in the city. Its mills produce more flour than any other U.S. city except Buffalo, New York. Kansas City's workers also produce chemicals, clothes, automobile parts, farm machinery, fiber optics, and soap.

transporting industrial products. Tourism is also booming in the area. Camping and hiking are popular pastimes, and the river and lakes provide plenty of outdoor recreation, such as canoeing, sport fishing, and water skiing.

But the natural landscape and wildlife of the Missouri River have suffered as a result of these changes. Animals and plants that once thrived by the Missouri River now find it difficult to survive. In the last fifty years, the river's fishing harvests have dropped by as much as 80 percent, and it is now illegal to catch some native species. As it is with other North American rivers, it is difficult to strike a balance between the needs of the Missouri's people and its environment.

Below: *Downtown Kansas City is on the south side of the Missouri River.*

5 Places to Visit

Along the Missouri's long, winding course, visitors can see everything from historical sites to Native monuments to areas of natural beauty.

❶ Gates of the Mountains, MT
Explorers Lewis and Clark first floated beneath these towering cliffs in July 1805. Today, people visit the Gates of the Mountains by boat or by hiking through the surrounding area.

❷ Little Bighorn National Monument, MT
The Battle of the Little Bighorn took place on June 25 and 26, 1876. Troops from the U.S. Cavalry clashed with Sioux, Cheyenne, and

Arapaho warriors under the command of Sitting Bull. Colonel George Custer and his men were all killed. The last few U.S. troops made the now famous "last stand" on Last Stand Hill, where today there is a memorial to them and the Native fighters who also died.

❸ Fort Mandan Overlook, ND
This site overlooks the area where Lewis and Clark's expedition set up camp across the river

from Native villages during the winter of 1804–1805. They named the site Fort Mandan in honor of their Native hosts. Here, Lewis and Clark met a French mountain man called Toussaint Charbonneau and his Shoshone wife Sacagawea. The couple traveled with Lewis and Clark on the rest of their journey to the Pacific Ocean.

④ Sitting Bull Burial Site, SD

Standing Rock Indian Reservation is home to the original burial site of the Sioux leader Sitting Bull (below). Sitting Bull defeated Colonel Custer at Little Bighorn. In 1890, Sitting Bull was killed by police attempting to arrest him at his home on the Grand River. He was buried in a cemetery on the edge of a military fort. A large boulder now marks this site. In 1953, Sitting Bull's remains were moved across the river to Mobridge, South Dakota.

⑤ Big Bend Dam, SD
Big Bend Dam was finished in 1966. It provides flood control, irrigation water, and electricity for more than 95,000 homes. The dam takes its name from the large bend in the river a few miles upstream from the dam.

⑥ Tarbox Hollow Living Prairie, NE
Tarbox Hollow Living Prairie is a small bison ranch. The ranch sells bison meat and wool, and the animals are supplied to other ranches all over North America.

⑦ Great Plains Black History Museum, NE
This museum was set up in 1976 to commemorate the history of African Americans in the West and the United States as a whole. Malcolm X (right), a Nation of Islam minister and one of the country's most influential African-American leaders, was born in Omaha in 1925.

⑧ Big Muddy National Fish and Wildlife Refuge, MO
This nature preserve covers about 12.5 square miles (32 sq km) of the Missouri River floodplain and surrounding areas. Conservationists are working to restore even more of the floodplain, all the way from Kansas City to St. Louis.

⑨ Harry S. Truman Reservoir State Park, MO
The Harry S. Truman Dam—named in honor of the former president from Independence, Missouri—is on the Osage River, a major tributary of the Missouri River. When it was completed in 1979, the dam created the Harry S. Truman Reservoir, which boasts some of the finest fishing in the state of Missouri. The Harry S. Truman State Park forms a peninsula that juts into the reservoir. The park is used for camping, picnics, and nature study.

⑩ Laclede's Landing, MO
Laclede's Landing is named after the French fur trapper Pierre Laclède, who, along with Auguste Choteau, founded the trading post of St. Louis in the 1760s. The area (right) is the oldest part of St. Louis. Its cobblestone streets are lined with refurbished nineteenth-century warehouses that once stored coffee, leather, tobacco, and whiskey.

How Rivers Form

Rivers have many features that are constantly changing in shape. The illustration below shows how these features are created.

Rivers flow from mountains to oceans, receiving water from rain, melting snow, and underground springs. Rivers collect their water from an area called the river basin. High mountain ridges form the divides between river basins.

Tributaries join the main river at places called confluences. Rivers flow down steep mountain slopes quickly but slow as they near the ocean and gather more water. Slow rivers have many meanders (wide turns) and often change course.

Near the mouth, levees (piles of mud) build up on the banks. The levees stop water from draining into the river, creating areas of swamp.

1 Glacier: An ice mass that melts into river water.

2 Lake: The source of many rivers; may be fed by springs or precipitation.

3 Rapids: Shallow water that flows quickly.

4 Waterfall: Formed when a river wears away softer rock, making a step in the riverbed.

5 Canyon: Formed when a river cuts a channel through rock.

6 Floodplain: A place where rivers often flood flat areas, depositing mud.

7 Oxbow lake: River bend cut off when a river changes course, leaving water behind.

8 Estuary: River mouth where river and ocean water mix together.

9 Delta: Triangular river mouth created when mud islands form, splitting the flow into several channels called distributaries.

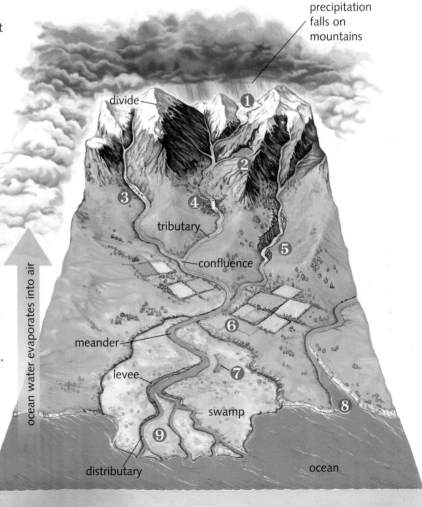

Glossary

agriculture The practice of growing crops and raising livestock as an industry.

barge A flat-bottomed boat used to transport goods and usually pulled or pushed by a tug.

basin The area drained by a river and its tributaries.

canal A man-made waterway used for navigation or irrigation.

cargo Transported products or merchandise.

confluence The place where rivers meet.

conservation Protection of natural resources and the environment

dam A constructed barrier across a river that controls the flow of water.

irrigation Watering crops with water from a river, lake, or other source.

levee A raised bank along a river that helps prevent flooding.

migration A regular journey undertaken by a group of animals from one climate to another for feeding and breeding purposes.

prairie Vast areas of grassland.

reservation An area of land set aside for a particular purpose. Many Natives live on reservations created by the government.

reservoir An artificial lake where water is stored for later use.

source The place where a river begins.

tributary A river that flows into a larger one at a confluence.

valley A hollow channel cut by a river usually between hills or mountains.

For Further Information

Books

Collier, Christopher and James Lincoln Collier. *Indians, Cowboys and Farmers: 1865–1910.* Marshall Cavendish, 2000.

Gunderson, Mary. *Cooking on the Lewis and Clark Expedition.* Capstone Press, 1999.

Lourie, Peter. *In the Path of Lewis and Clark.* Silver Burdett Press, 1996.

Roop, Peter. *Off the Map: The Journals of Lewis and Clark.* Walker and Company, 1998.

Web Sites

American Rivers
www.amrivers.org/missouririver/default.htm

Missouri River InfoLink
infolink.cr.usgs.gov

Missouri River Issues
www.dnr.state.mo.us/riverissues.htm

Pick–Sloan Missouri Basin Program
www.gp.usbr.gov/archive/glimpse/picksloan.htm

Index